A Note to Parents

DK READERS is a compelling program for beginning readers, designed in conjunction with leading literacy experts, including Dr. Linda Gambrell, Professor of Education at Clemson University. Dr. Gambrell has served as President of the National Reading Conference, the College Reading Association, and the International Reading Association.

Beautiful illustrations and superb full-color photographs combine with engaging, easy-to-read stories and informational texts to offer a fresh approach to each subject in the series. Each DK READER is guaranteed to capture a child's interest while developing his or her reading skills, general knowledge, and love of reading.

The five levels of DK READERS are aimed at different reading abilities, enabling you to choose the books that are exactly right for your child:

Pre-level 1: Learning to read
Level 1: Beginning to read
Level 2: Beginning to read alone
Level 3: Reading alone
Level 4: Proficient readers

The "normal" age at which a child begins to read can be anywhere from three to eight years old. Adult participation through the lower levels is very helpful for providing encouragement, discussing storylines, and sounding out unfamiliar words.

No matter which level you select, you can be sure that you are helping your child learn to read, then read to learn!

LONDON, NEW YORK, MUNICH,
MELBOURNE, AND DELHI

For DK/BradyGames
Global Strategy Guide Publisher
Mike Degler
Digital and Trade Category Publisher
Brian Saliba
Licensing Manager
Christian Sumner
Editor-In-Chief
H. Leigh Davis
Operations Manager
Stacey Beheler
Title Manager
Tim Fitzpatrick
Book Designer
Tim Amrhein
Production Designer
Areva

For DK Publishing
Publishing Director
Beth Sutinis
Licensing Editor
Nancy Ellwood
Reading Consultant
Linda B. Gambrell, Ph.D.

DK/BradyGAMES

800 East 96th St., 3rd floor

Indianapolis, IN 46240

11 12 13 10 9 8 7 6 5 4 3 2 1

A catalog record for this book is available from the Library of Congress.

ISBN: 978-0-7566-5394-1 (Paperback)

ISBN: 978-0-7566-8701-4 (Hardback)

Printed and bound by Lake Book Manufacturing, Inc.

Discover more at
www.dk.com

Contents

 **READERS**

READING
3
ALONE

Ash Battles
His Rivals!

Written by Simcha Whitehill

DK Publishing

Meet Ash and Pikachu

When Ash Ketchum was 10 years old, he set off from his home in Pallet Town on an epic journey to become a Pokémon Trainer. With Pikachu, his first Pokémon, always by his side, Ash has battled through several regions, making friends along the way!

Ash brought Pikachu, his first Pokémon, with him on his journey.

When Ash ventured to the Sinnoh region, he took on every challenge the region had to offer. He entered Gym battles and earned eight badges. This gave him a chance to compete against all of his rivals in a region-wide showdown called the Sinnoh League tournament!

In the pages of this book, you will discover how Ash prepared for his biggest battles in a brand new region, against a whole new group of tough competitors: Nando, Barry, Conway, and his fiercest rival, Paul.

Welcome to Sinnoh!

Sinnoh is an amazing place to visit! From the big cities, to the lush forests, to the sparkling seas, Sinnoh is a paradise for people who love Pokémon.

If you like the bustle of busy sidewalks, Sinnoh city life can't be beat! Each town has something special to attract people and Pokémon alike. Floaroma Town is covered in sweet-smelling flowers. Eterna City's awesome museum has lots of precious artifacts. In Jubilife City, you can shop 'til you drop.

The coastal metropolis of Sunyshore City.

Ash, Brock, and Dawn survey the scenic beauty of Lake Acuity.

Sinnoh also offers a lot to nature lovers. There are plenty of great places to see Pokémon in the wild. Must-see nature spots include a 1,000-year-old tree that many Pokémon call home; the Valley Path, where Flying-types soar in flocks; and the beautiful Eterna Forest, home to many honey-making Combee.

Meet Dawn

At the beginning of Ash's journey through Sinnoh, friendly Dawn helped him locate his lost Pikachu. From then on, they were great pals! Dawn takes good care of her Pokémon. She doesn't like having a hair out of place, and she's just as concerned about her Pokémon grooming. Dawn is dedicated to being beautiful, both inside and out. Dawn travels with Ash and Brock through Sinnoh!

Piplup was Dawn's first Pokémon.

Meet Brock

The former Gym Leader in Pewter City, Brock has been Ash's friend since Ash's early days as a Trainer in Kanto. Brock is a good travel buddy because he cooks delicious meals and is always there for Ash in a pinch. Brock has worked hard to be an awesome Pokémon breeder, but he is easily distracted by girls.

The first Pokémon Brock caught in the Sinnoh region was Croagunk.

Meet Some of the Villains

Team Rocket

This troublesome trio is made up of Jessie, James, and a talking Meowth. While their job is to steal Pokémon, they think they can really impress their

Team Rocket followed Ash from Kanto to Sinnoh.

boss, Giovanni, by nabbing Ash's Pikachu.

Team Galactic

This highly organized team of Sinnoh villains is interested in high-stakes scores and high-tech gadgets. Team Galactic's leader, Cyrus, relies heavily on his star workers: Saturn, Mars, Jupiter, and Charon.

Saturn, Mars, Cyrus, and Jupiter of Team Galactic.

Nando

Now that you know Ash and his friends, it's time to meet Ash's rivals! Nando, the Pokémon bard, carries a golden harp shaped like Mew. As he strums, sweet rhymes roll off his tongue. Nando's gentle style is unlike most competitive Trainers. In fact, he wasn't sure whether to be a Trainer or a Coordinator until Ash and Dawn battled him. Then he saw that he could be both.

See the next page to learn which Pokémon Nando has on hand in Sinnoh!

Nando favors Bug-type and Grass-type Pokémon.

Nando's Pokémon

Armaldo

Type: Rock Bug

Height: 4'11"   **Weight:** 150.4 lbs

Fun Facts: Armaldo comes from a prehistoric species of Pokémon.

Nando battled with Armaldo against Ash and Quilava in the Sinnoh League Tournament. Find out what happened on page 15.

Budew

Type: Grass Poison

Height: 0' 08"   **Weight:** 2.6 lbs.

Fun Facts: Budew bloom in spring, but look out because their pollen might just make you sneeze!

During Ash and Pikachu's first battle with Nando, Budew evolved into Roselia. When Ash saw Nando later at the Sinnoh League Tournament, it had evolved again into Roserade!

Kricketune

Type: Bug

Height: 3'03"   **Weight:** 56.2 lbs.

Fun Facts: Kricketune is a Pokémon whose melodies pack a powerful attack punch.

Nando's musical Kricketune has a fine-tuned Sing move and often harmonizes with Sunflora's Grasswhistle.

Sunflora

Type: Grass

Height: 2'07"   **Weight:** 18.7 lbs.

Fun Facts: The sun's rays make Sunflora grow even stronger.

Nando and Sunflora once stopped Ash and Dawn from arguing by performing a bright display of Sunny Day.

Nando Meets Ash!

Nando first meets Ash in the forest. Nando notices that Ash and Dawn are arguing, so he tells Sunflora to shine a bright Sunny Day to make them happy again.

Eager to make cool new friends, Ash, Dawn, and Brock introduce themselves to Nando. Dawn and Ash each challenge him to a battle. During Ash's match, Nando's Budew evolves into a Roselia. However, Ash and Pikachu win the battle.

Nando is such a nice guy, it's almost hard to believe that he is Ash's and Dawn's rival!

Nando's Budew evolved into a Roselia.

At the Sinnoh Historical Museum, tricky Team Rocket has disguised Meowth as Sunflora. They hope to steal the amazing Adamant Orb.

Because Nando travels with Sunflora, Officer Jenny mistakes him for the thief and arrests him. Ash, Dawn, and Brock stand by Nando! With Pikachu and Piplup's help, Nando's Sunflora finds Team Rocket and helps prove Nando's innocence. Nando thanks Ash, Dawn, and Brock for helping him. True friends are the ones you can count on when the going gets tough.

Sunflora helped foil Team Rocket's plan to steal the Adamant Orb.

Later, Ash and his pal Nando are set to battle each other in the Sinnoh League tournament's first round. At the start, the sweet scent of Nando's Roserade softens Ash's Staraptor. However, Ash's Staraptor wins the round with a soaring Brave Bird.

Next, Ash sends Quilava against Nando's Armaldo. Both Pokémon get knocked out and the round ends in a tie.

For their final Pokémon, Nando's Kricketune puts Ash's Heracross to

Ash's Quilava battles to a draw against Nando's Armaldo.

sleep. However, Ash has Heracross use Sleep Talk to pound a surprise Focus Punch. Heracross comes back to win for Ash!

Always a good sport, Nando thanks Ash for these three incredible battles.

Ash's confident battle style helps Nando see how important it is to be true to himself. Nando learns that he can follow his dreams and be both a Coordinator and a Trainer.

Despite an early setback, Heracross pulls off the win!

Conway always looks for new angles to win battles.

Conway

A calculating Trainer, Conway is always figuring out a formula to win, especially against his rival, Ash. Despite his brainpower, Conway spends much of his time creeping around to spy on the competition. This smug Trainer has a soft spot for Dawn. So, he keeps trying to impress Dawn with his secrets, but she doesn't care about his shady information. Besides, no matter how much he spies on Ash, it doesn't seem to help him on the battlefield!

Conway's Pokémon

Slowking

Type: Water Psychic

Height: 6'07" **Weight:** 175.3 lbs.

Fun Facts: That crown on Slowking's head is actually a Shellder. Slowking is Conway's favorite Pokémon.

Heracross

Type: Bug Fighting

Height: 4'11" **Weight:** 119.0 lbs.

Fun Facts: Using the sharp claws on its feet, Heracross digs into bark so it can hurl foes with its horn.

In the Hearthome City Tag Team Competition, Conway's Heracross impressed fans with a radical Revenge that doubled its attack strength.

Shuckle

Type: Bug Rock

Height: 2'00" **Weight:** 45.2 lbs.

Fun Facts: Shuckle blends berries in its shell to turn them into a yummy juice.

Conway's Shuckle can turn its defensive power into attack power with its terrific Power Trick.

Lickilicky

Type: Normal

Height: 5'07" **Weight:** 308.6 lbs.

Fun Facts: Lickilicky can tie up opponents with its long tongue.

Conway's Lickilicky has a highly trained tongue that can pack quite a Power Whip.

Dusknoir

Type: Ghost

Height: 7'03" **Weight:** 235.0 lbs.

Fun Facts: Dusknoir uses the yellow antenna on its head to communicate with the spirit world.

Conway's Dusknoir can fence Pokémon in a force field by using Trick Room.

Conway Meets Ash!

At the Tag Battle Competition in Hearthome City, Conway and Dawn are teammates. They make it to the finals to face the team of Ash and his other rival, prideful Paul!

Although they don't work together, Ash and Paul manage to defeat Conway and Dawn. In the middle of the match, Paul's Elekid evolves into Electabuzz.

Paul's Elekid evolved into Electabuzz in mid-battle!

With help from Ash's Chimchar, Electabuzz takes Conway's team out of the battle. Despite their differences, Ash and Paul win the whole tournament!

On another occasion, Ash, Brock, and Dawn run into Conway at Professor Rowan's Summer Academy.

Professor Rowan runs a summer academy for Pokémon Trainers.

Lumineon received unwanted attention from "Jessilinda."

In one activity, Conway follows Ash, Dawn, and Brock when they try to find a Lumineon that's luring Pokémon with its light. However, Team Rocket's Jessie, disguised as "Jessilinda," shows up to catch Lumineon.

Conway stands up for his friends, calling on Slowking to battle Jessilinda and Yanmega. Ash, Dawn, and Brock thank him for his help—Conway is just happy that Dawn notices his cool battle skills!

Jessie disguised herself as "Jessilinda."

Though they're all rivals on the battlefield, they still look out for each other like good friends should.

Jessie sent Yanmega to battle Conway's Slowking.

Ash and Conway meet again as rivals in the Sinnoh League tournament.

Conway spied on Ash during practice.

Sneaky Conway spies on Ash's practice so he can learn his moves. Conway thinks Ash will use the three Pokémon he has out: Infernape, Torterra, and Glalie. However, Ash surprises Conway at their match by choosing Noctowl, Donphan, and Gible. Despite Conway's spying and his calculating moves, Ash wins the battle!

Although Ash practiced with Glalie, he used different Pokémon for the match.

The one thing Conway didn't predict is that Ash is unpredictable. Unlike Conway, who prepares a formula to win before the round, Ash makes his decisions on the fly. He is always

Donphan was part of Ash's unpredictable battle team.

full of surprises, and that can be just as successful as Conway's methodical battle style!

Ash's winning Pokémon celebrate with a meal!

Barry

Blonde-haired Barry is always bouncing off the walls. This turbocharged Trainer loves to brag about himself, but he really idolizes Ash's biggest rival, Paul. At first, Barry teased Ash for not being able to beat Paul in battle. Nevertheless, Ash gladly helped Barry out of a few sticky situations. That helped Ash and Barry grow to be good friends as well as rivals. Still, this doesn't stop impatient Barry from trying to fine Ash when he doesn't get his way!

Barry looks up to Paul, one of Ash's greatest rivals.

Palmer

Barry's father, Palmer, is known around Twinleaf Town as the "Tower Tycoon." He's the leader of the Battle Tower arena.

Palmer and his son, Barry.

Barry wants to grow up to be as great as his dad, but he is already like Palmer in so many ways. They're both spirited, snappy, and possess big personalities. No one can match Palmer's superstar battle style— he can really get the crowd cheering!

Barry's Pokémon

Empoleon

Type: Steel Water
Height: 5'07" **Weight:** 186.3 lbs.

Fun Facts: Regal and full of pride, you can tell how powerful Empoleon is by the size of the horns on its head.

Barry's Empoleon can do a mean Hyper Beam.

Staraptor

Type: Normal Flying
Height: 3'11" **Weight:** 54.9 lbs.

Fun Facts: Staraptor isn't afraid to boldly challenge much bigger Pokémon.

Both Ash and Barry have Staraptor on hand to battle in Sinnoh.

Roserade

Type: Grass Poison
Height: 2'11" **Weight:** 32.0 lbs.

Fun Facts: Its sweet scent tricks its foes into getting close so Roserade can get them in its thorny clutches.

Nando and Barry both have Roserade with serious flower power.

Ash Battles Barry!

As Ash walks up the Hearthome City Gym's steps to challenge Fantina to a rematch, Barry runs him over. Upon this first meeting, Barry tries to fine Ash for bumping into the boy he thinks will become the strongest Trainer in the world—himself. Barry then runs off in a hurry, dropping his three badges. Ash wants to return Barry's badge case. Fantina tells him he can find Barry at the Pokémon Center, because he just lost their Gym battle.

On the way to the Pokémon Center, Barry slams into Ash again. This time, he recognizes Ash as being Paul's partner in the Hearthome City Tag Battle competition. Dawn tells Barry she knows him because they're both from Twinleaf Town.

However, Barry says he remembers her and Brock only as the geeks who lost to Paul in the Tag Team competition. Barry really looks up to Paul, and he teases Ash, Dawn, and Brock for not being able to beat Paul in battle. Barry's rude attitude makes Ash want to show him what he's made of on the battlefield!

The result of Ash's and Barry's run in!

Barry accepts Ash's challenge! Ash wins the battle's first matchup. However, Barry then identifies Ash's Chimchar as the one that Paul had. Barry

Pikachu brings home a win for Ash!

knows how to defeat Chimchar from watching it in the Tag Battle, so he wins the second round. In the final round, Ash's Pikachu stays strong against Barry's Empoleon, winning the battle!

Sore loser Barry tells Ash that he's still the better Pokémon Trainer. Ash invites Barry to watch him win his rematch against Fantina at the Hearthome City Gym.

As promised, Barry shows up to watch Ash's rematch with Fantina for the Relic Badge. Fantina's Psychic-types are known for their powerful Hypnosis, but Ash is prepared. He has his Pokémon combine two attacks to act together

Mismagius is one of Fantina's three Pokémon in this rematch.

defensively and offensively. Thanks to his creative strategy, Ash earns his fifth badge in Sinnoh!

Barry is surprised at Ash's win. He says he's off to Iron Island to train for a match at the nearby Canalave Gym. Ash offers to accompany his rival to Canalave Gym. Barry agrees, but he says that he won't consider Ash competition unless he wins the Mine Badge there.

During a Pokémon Center visit in Canalave City, Ash gets a distress call from Barry. All the Steel-type Pokémon on Iron Island have gone berserk, including Barry's Empoleon. Ash tells Barry that he and his friends are on their way!

When they arrive, a storm of crazed Steel-types is chasing Barry and Heracross. A low-frequency

Barry's Empoleon went berserk, along with the other Steel-type Pokémon!

wave is causing this Pokémon problem. The wave originates from a machine placed at the shrine to the Legendary Pokémon Dialga and Palkia. Someone is trying to uncover the Sinnoh Space-Time Legend and they must be stopped!

Barry finds the machine, along with Team Rocket, but they're not to blame. Mars and her fellow Team Galactic goons are controlling the machine. In order to defeat them, the kids must join forces with Team Rocket!

Quick-thinking Ash chooses Staravia to fly Pikachu to the machine and destroy it with Thunderbolt. Iron Island is safe again! Happy that they put their differences aside for the greater good, Barry thanks Ash for his help.

Staravia helped Pikachu destroy the trouble-making machine.

The next time these rivals meet, Ash is trying to catch a wild Gible. Barry soon decides that he wants to beat Ash at catching it.

Despite Barry's efforts, Ash caught the wild Gible.

The race is on, and even Team Rocket tries to steal Gible! However, Pikachu blasts them off, and Ash finally has the chance to catch it.

In response, Barry and Empoleon challenge Ash and Gible to a battle. During the battle, Gible doesn't follow Ash's instructions, and Empoleon easily wins. Barry has the upper hand for now, but the big Sinnoh League competition is just around the corner.

Unfortunately, Paul knocks Barry out of the running before he gets the chance to battle Ash again.

Paul

Ash's greatest rival is Paul, his polar opposite. Paul isn't afraid to say exactly what he thinks, no matter how mean it is. This ultra-competitive Trainer doesn't care about making friends; Paul is only happy when he wins. Strict and a tough judge, Paul often throws back Pokémon he catches and tells them they're weak.

Paul is strict and a tough judge.

33

In fact, Ash wound up asking Chimchar to join him on his journey after Paul abandoned it. While powerful Paul can be harsh at times, it's all part of his battle strategy to avoid feelings and rely on strength.

Because Ash and Paul are so unlike each other, they actually form a perfect balance

Ash and Paul have opposite battle styles.

in battle. According to Cynthia, they will become a very important match someday. Cynthia tells Ash and Paul their destiny by quoting the Sinnoh Space-Time Legend: "When every life meets another life, something will be born…"

While her message is confusing, Ash and Paul know their battles hold some higher purpose. As they first compete against each other in Sinnoh, their fate begins...

Cynthia

As the Champion of Sinnoh, Cynthia is highly

Cynthia believes that Ash's and Paul's destinies are linked.

respected. She is also an expert on the Legendary Pokémon Dialga and Palkia. She sees Paul and Ash as important rivals whose battles have a mystical meaning.

Paul and his brother, Reggie.

Reggie

Paul couldn't be more different from his brother Reggie! Reggie is a kind, laid-back, and friendly Pokémon breeder who lives in Veilstone City. Despite their differences, Reggie is always there to cheer on Paul and even make friends with his rivals, like Ash.

Paul's Pokémon

Aggron

Type: Steel Rock

Height: 6'11" **Weight:** 793.7 lbs.

Fun Facts: Aggron's horns are so strong they can break through bedrock.

Aggron was the first Pokémon Paul used in his six-on-six battle against Ash in the Sinnoh League.

Chimchar

Type: Fire

Height: 1'08" **Weight:** 13.7 lbs.

Fun Facts: Rain can't put out the flame on the tip of its tail, but it stops burning when Chimchar sleeps.

When Paul first met Chimchar, he watched it battle back a bunch of Zangoose. Paul tried to bring out that same fire in Chimchar by putting it in very stressful situations, but it never worked. When Paul got sick of Chimchar and let it go, Ash stepped in to adopt the powerful Pokémon. With a good friend like Ash, Chimchar evolved first into Monferno and then into Infernape.

Drapion

Type: Poison Dark

Height: 4'03" **Weight:** 135.6 lbs.

Fun Facts: Drapion is known for its poisonous attacks, but it can also crush a car in its claws.

During the Sinnoh League quarterfinals, Paul asked Drapion to use Poison Spikes on the battlefield. It was such a strong move that Ash's Pokémon were still being poisoned when they stepped onto the field during later matchups.

Electabuzz

Type: Electric

Height: 3'07" **Weight:** 66.1 lbs.

Fun Facts: Electabuzz love to eat up all the electricity that power plants have to offer. In fact, they cause 50% of blackouts!

Paul's Elekid evolved into Electabuzz during the final round of the Hearthome City Tag Battle Competition.

Froslass

Type: Ice Ghost

Height: 4'03"   **Weight:** 58.6 lbs.

Fun Facts: Froslass' frosty breath can turn its enemies into icicles.

Paul's Froslass brought a blizzard to the Sinnoh League battle arena.

Torterra

Type: Grass Ground

Height: 7'03"   **Weight:** 683.4 lbs.

Fun Facts: Smaller Pokémon like to make their homes on Torterra's back.

Before it ever battled Ash's Pokémon, Paul's Turtwig reached its fully evolved form, Torterra. It can blast an incredible Hyper Beam.

Ursaring

Type: Normal

Height: 5'11"   **Weight:** 277.3 lbs.

Fun Facts: Ursaring marks trees that have delicious berries by clawing on their bark.

Paul caught Ursaring as it chased Ash, Dawn, and Brock in Bewilder Forest.

Ash Faces Paul!

When Ash steps off the ferry in Sinnoh, Team Rocket steals Pikachu. Ash and Brock follow the trio's hot air balloon into the woods, looking for lost Pikachu.

There, they run into Paul trying to catch a flock of Starly with Elekid. Picky Paul captures three Starly, but he only keeps the one he thinks is the best.

Paul challenges Ash to a three-on-three battle. Without Pikachu, Ash has only two on hand. Paul calls Ash pathetic and then he leaves. Ash doesn't understand why Paul is so cruel.

After Ash reunites with Pikachu, they head to Professor Rowan's lab where they find Paul waiting for them. Now Ash is ready for Paul's three-on-three battle!

The first round is a head-to-head battle between Ash's Starly and Paul's Starly. Paul wins, but he still teases his Starly, saying, "Is that the best you could do?"

Next, Ash chooses Aipom to battle Paul's Chimchar. Aipom wins with a powerful Focus Punch.

Now it's up to the final round to decide the winner.

Ash chooses Pikachu to battle Paul and Elekid. Clever Paul turns Pikachu's Thunderbolt against it, powering up Elekid's Thunder. It's such an even match that Elekid and Pikachu are both unable to continue. Brock calls a tie.

As a good sport, Ash says that Paul is the winner because Pikachu passed out first. Paul doesn't care. As he walks away, he throws back Starly and calls it weak. Paul doesn't make a good first impression on Ash!

Paul treats his newly caught Starly harshly.

Ash bumps into Paul again on his way to Oreburgh City, and he wants a rematch. Just as Ash and Paul get started, Team Rocket steals Ash's Turtwig! Paul has his Chimchar use Ember, and Ash's Pikachu blasts them off with Thunderbolt.

However, as Turtwig is returned to Ash, a strong wind blows the battlers off a cliff and into a lake.

Ash and Turtwig then wander into Bewilder Forest. Little do they know, if they lock eyes with the wild Stantler that live there, they'll fall into a dreamy sleep. Paul soon finds Ash and Turtwig sleepwalking. Paul sends in Chimchar to catch the Stantler that's bothering Ash.

When Ash wakes up, Paul teases him, releases the Stantler, and then leaves.

On a separate occasion, as a giant Ursaring chases Ash, Dawn, and Brock, they run into Paul again. Chimchar uses Flame Wheel to help Paul catch Ursaring. Ash thanks Paul for the help and offers to battle again.

In the rematch, Paul once again defeats Ash. Paul taunts Ash for losing and then leaves. Just then, Ash vows to work hard so he'll never lose to his rival Paul again.

A Stantler in Bewilder Forest put Ash and Turtwig to sleep!

At the Hearthome City Tag Battle Competition, Ash is randomly paired up with Paul. Paul is not happy to be partnered with Ash, so he tells Ash to stay out of his way.

Halfway through the competition, Paul angrily abandons Chimchar for being afraid of an opposing Zangoose. Ash steps up to help both Chimchar and Turtwig win the round by working together. Afterward, Paul tells Chimchar to get lost. Luckily, Ash is there to ask Chimchar to join him and his friends.

Zangoose frightened Chimchar!

Even when Ash and Paul make it to the finals, Paul again refuses to play nice. They're up against Conway and Heracross with Dawn and Buizel. Ash chooses Chimchar and Paul chooses Elekid. At first, it looks like Ash and Paul are going to lose because they aren't listening to each other. However, in the middle of the match, Elekid suddenly evolves into Electabuzz. This gives them the extra power they need to win. Ash and Paul are champions, but Paul angrily throws his trophy at Ash and storms away. Even when Paul wins, he is still a bad sport.

Elekid's Evolution saved the match!

Paul's brother Reggie sets up a full six-on-six battle for Ash and Paul at Lake Acuity. The beginning doesn't go Ash's way, and he has only one Pokémon still standing: Chimchar, which used to belong to Paul. Meanwhile, Paul has five Pokémon still able to battle.

Though Ash cannot hope to beat these odds, Chimchar shows Paul how hard it has been training. Not only does it defeat Paul's Ursaring, it evolves into an amazingly strong Monferno!

Ash's Chimchar evolved into Monferno during the match!

Still, Paul wins his first full battle against Ash. However, Ash knows they'll meet again...

The next time Ash sees Paul, they're about to battle in the Sinnoh League tournament's high-stakes quarterfinals. Their rivalry is so important, even Champion Cynthia watches the battle.

Before the match, Paul gets pumped up with a pep talk from his brother, Reggie. Ash, on the other hand, focuses on practice. Ash wants to show he has learned from his mistakes in their previous battle at Lake Acuity.

During the contest, it becomes clear that he is using the exact same Pokémon he chose at Lake Acuity. However, the moves are not the same.

Infernape landed the winning blow for Ash!

The epic six-on-six match takes Paul and Ash down to their very last Pokémon. The fury of the final attacks erupts into a windstorm. In the end, Infernape wins the entire match for Ash with a blast of Fire Blitz!

Ash is proud that he has finally shown Paul the value of his training style. While Paul thought that all he needed were strong Pokémon to win, Ash proved that strength can also come from friendship. It seems that Ash has earned more than just a place in the Sinnoh League's next round—he has also won Paul's respect.

Conclusion

While Ash must battle many rivals on his journey to become a Pokémon Master, he can still welcome them as friends off the field. Ash's positive attitude, loyalty, and good sportsmanship have made him an awesome Trainer as well as a great friend. So, as Ash continues his travels, there is no doubt that a lot of stiff competition and new pals lie ahead!

Glossary

academy
school; college; society of persons organized to advance art, science, or literature

accompany
to escort; to go with

bard
a poet or singer skilled in writing and performing verses

berserk
wild; crazy; out of control

bustle
activity; movement; commotion

calculating
shrewd; cunning; scheming

distress
worry; pain; trouble; difficulty

impatient
anxious; hurried; rash

innocence
freedom from guilt; blamelessness; virtue

methodical
careful; precise; deliberate

metropolis
any large or busy city

pathetic
useless; pitiful; feeble

opposite
contrary; reverse; converse

quarterfinal
one of four matches, games, or contests to decide the four people or teams that will continue playing in a competition

region
area; section; territory; district

rival
opponent; competitor; foe; adversary

shady
underhanded; suspicious; shifty; dishonest

showdown
confrontation; fight; conflict

sportsmanship
fairness; respect for one's opponent; graciousness in winning or losing; conduct appropriate for one who participates in a sport

tournament
contest; competition; match; a series of games or contests that make up a single unit of competition

tycoon
a businessperson of exceptional wealth and power; a top leader